FALL
Clip Art A La Carte

Concept and compilation
by
Imogene Forte

Incentive Publications, Inc.
Nashville, Tennessee

Cover by Susan Eaddy
Designed by Dianna Richey

ISBN 0-86530-200-6

Table of Contents

PREFACE iv

ILLUSTRATED USES OF THIS BOOK v
FALL POSTER/BOOKLET COVER 9
AUTUMN ANTICS...11
MONTHLY BANNERS 13
MONTHLY BANNERS 15
AWARDS AND INCENTIVES 17
COMMUNICATORS AND MOTIVATORS 19
FALL FROLIC 21
SEPTEMBER BORDERS 23
SEPTEMBER'S SPECIAL DAYS 25
BACK TO SCHOOL 27
SCHOOL TOOLS 29
TRAFFIC AND SAFETY 31
SCHOOL SUBJECTS 33
BACK TO SCHOOL WITH MOTHER GOOSE 35
OCTOBER BORDERS 37
HALLOWEEN MINI ART 39
HALLOWEEN 41
JACK O' LANTERNS...43
FOR THE LOVE OF READING 45
SHIPS AND BOATS..47
NOVEMBER BORDERS 49
NOVEMBER MINI ART 51
PILGRIMS AND INDIANS 53
THANKSGIVING..55
FRUITS AND VEGETABLES 57
FINE FEATHERED FRIENDS 59
AUTUMN HARVEST..61
LEAVES 63
SEEDS 65
BUILDINGS 67
PERSONALITY ANIMALS 69
DIZZY DINOSAURS 71
NOTES 73
FALL ALPHABET 75

About This Book

The three books in the KIDS' STUFF™ CLIP ART A LA CARTE series (fall, winter, spring) were designed to meet the many requests we have had for a collection of our unique KIDS' STUFF™ art to communicate, motivate, and appeal to students, parents, and especially to teachers. It sounds easy, but you would not believe the many hours we spent adapting and thematically organizing the hundreds of publishers quality offerings in these books. The art on each page is printed on one side only to allow for selections to be clipped and used directly from the pages or for a photo copy to be made so that the books may be kept intact for future use.

The following 101 suggestions and the illustrated projects on pages 5-7 are provided to help you get started. So we invite you to clip, snip, and enjoy KIDS' STUFF™ CLIP ART A LA CARTE. It's that easy!

Activity Cards
Art Projects
Awards
Badges
Bag Decorations
Banners
Booklet Covers
Bookmarks
Book Plates
Borders
Bracelets
Brochures
Bulletin Boards
Bulletins
Calendars
Categorization
Chalkboard
  Projects
Charts
Collages:
  •Animals
  •Ecology
  •Exercise
  •Health
  •Holidays
  •Mother Goose
  •Reading
  •Safety
  •Seasons
  •Ships and Boats
  •Toys
  •Traffic
  •Weather
Communicators

Cutups
Desk Identifiers
Dioramas
Door Knob Hangers
Envelopes
Flip-Ups
Folder Decorations
Fold-Ups
Forms
Frames
Game Boards
Game Pieces
Gift Folders
Gifts
Gift Tags
Gift Wrap Decorations
Greeting Cards
Hang-ups
Headbands
Holiday Decorations
Homework Assignments
Incentives
Invitations
Jewelry
Journals
Labels
Learning Center
  Components
Library Aids
Locker Identification
Mailboxes
Mazes
Memos
Menus

Mini Art
Mini Books
Mobiles
Motivators
Name Tags
Napkin Rings
Necklaces
Notes
Party Favors
Paste-ups
Patterns
Pick-ups
Pins
Pin-ups
Place Cards
Posters
Pop-ups
Puppets
Puzzles
Record Forms
Review Sheets
Rhyme Booklets
Room Dividers
Signs
Stand-ups
Stencils
Stick-ups
Story Starters
String-ups
Student Contracts
Student Worksheets
Teacher's Records
Tokens
Tree Decorations
Window Decorations

stationery
Pg. 59

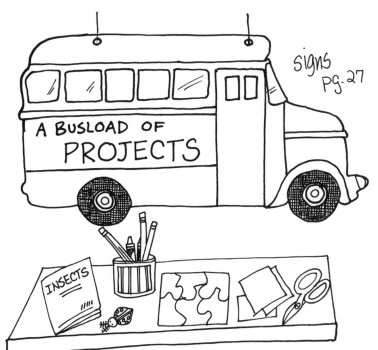

A BUSLOAD OF PROJECTS

INSECTS

signs
Pg. 27

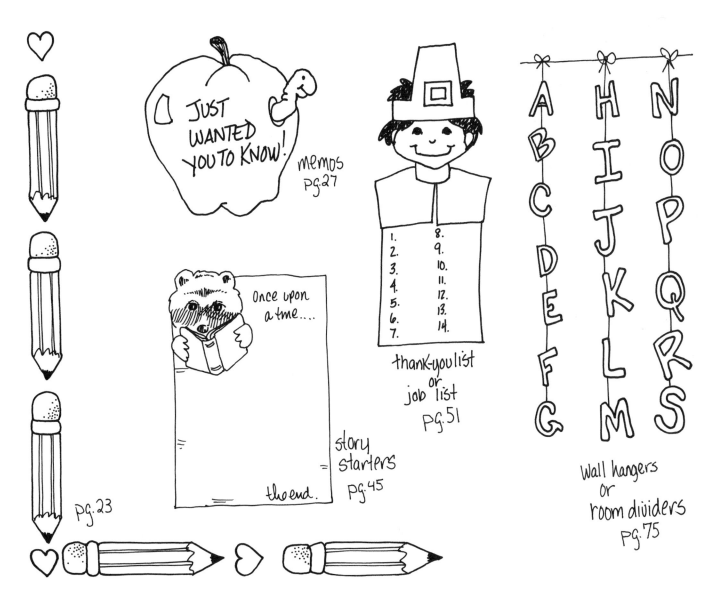

JUST WANTED YOU TO KNOW!

memos
Pg. 27

Once upon a time....

the end.

story starters
Pg. 45

thank-you list
or
job list
Pg. 51

A B C D E F G
H I J K L M
N O P Q R S

Wall hangers
or
room dividers
Pg. 75

Pg. 23

Traffic and Safety

STOP

NO PASSING ZONE

SCHOOL CROSSING

SLOW

CAUTION

mobiles
Pg. 31

MATH IX

notebook
covers
Pg. 33

Bobby

name
tags
Pg. 41

necklaces
Pg. 43

Read a scary story

bookmarks
Pg. 39

GOOD JOB !

awards
Pg. 33

stand-ups
pg. 67

finger
puppets
pg. 71

place cards
pg. 67

Charles

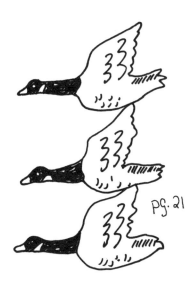

pg. 21

toby
5

frames
pg. 37

vii

FALL

AUTUMN ANTICS

SEPTEMBER

OCTOBER

NOVEMBER

AUTUMN SPLENDORS

WOW!

STAR STUDENT

FRIENDSHIP AWARD

Thank you

GOOD WORK

has something to crow about!

HAPPY BIRTHDAY

IS A

SAFETY SPECIALIST

COMMUNICATORS AND MOTIVATORS

My name is

_____

I'm on a field trip.

HI!

My name is _____

Welcome back,

It's That Time Again.

Please Come

VOTE

FALL FROLIC

SEPTEMBER'S SPECIAL DAYS

NATIVE AMERICAN DAY

LABOR DAY

Labor Day

GOOD CITIZENSHIP AWARD

CITIZENSHIP DAY

FIRST DAY OF AUTUMN

GRANDPARENTS' DAY

HAPPY GRANDPARENTS' DAY!

HAPPY GRANDPARENTS DAY

GOOD NEIGHBOR DAY

POP

NOTES

FIRST DAY OF SCHOOL

JOHNNY APPLESEED'S BIRTHDAY

BACK TO SCHOOL

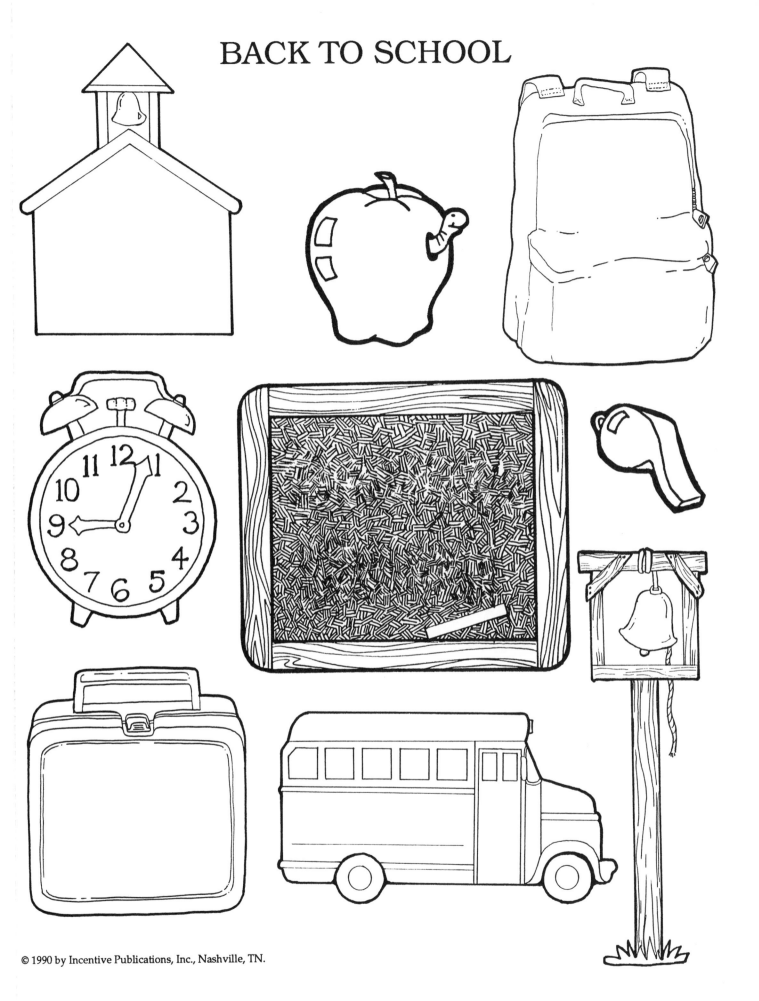

SCHOOL TOOLS

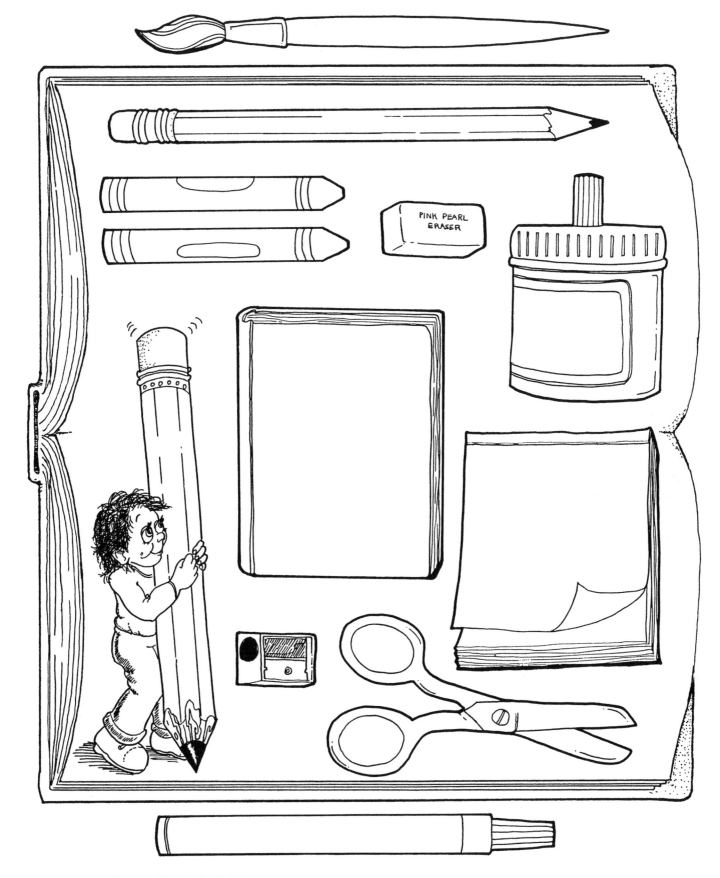

TRAFFIC AND SAFETY

NO PASSING ZONE

YIELD

SLOW

SCHOOL CROSSING

DO NOT ENTER

CAUTION

STOP

ONE WAY

SCHOOL SUBJECTS

BACK TO SCHOOL WITH MOTHER GOOSE

HALLOWEEN MINI ART

HALLOWEEN

JACK O' LANTERNS

FOR THE LOVE OF READING

Good Reader

NATIONAL CHILDREN'S BOOK WEEK

Webster's Dictionary

NOAH WEBSTER'S BIRTHDAY
(OCTOBER 16)

SHIPS AND BOATS

COLUMBUS DAY
(SECOND WEEK IN OCTOBER)

S.S. Good Citizenship

NOVEMBER MINI ART

PILGRIMS AND INDIANS

THANKSGIVING

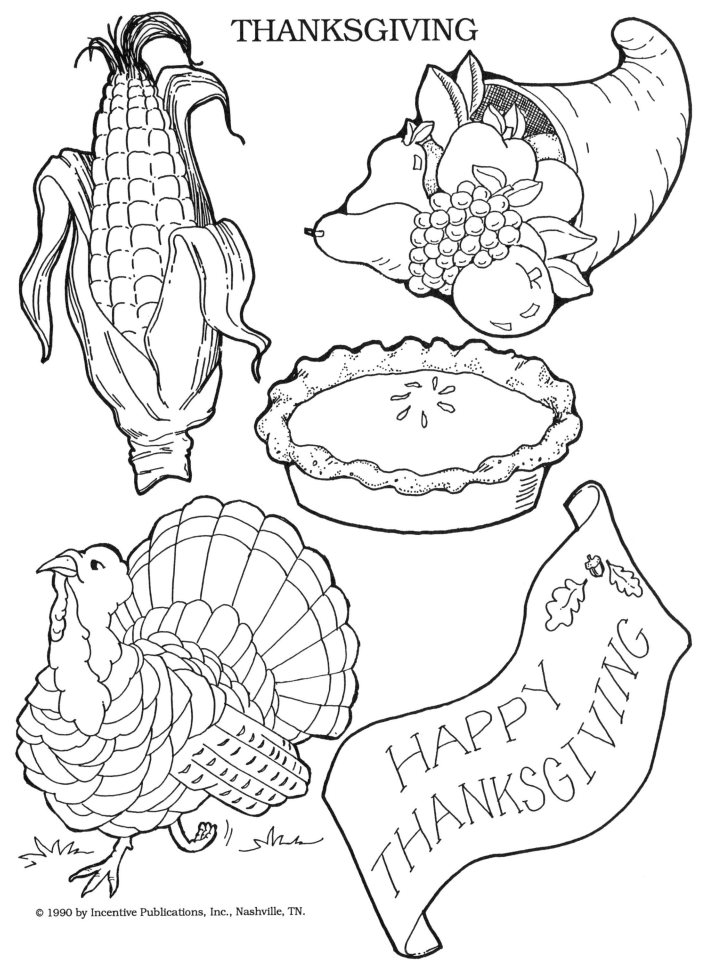

HAPPY THANKSGIVING

FRUITS AND VEGETABLES

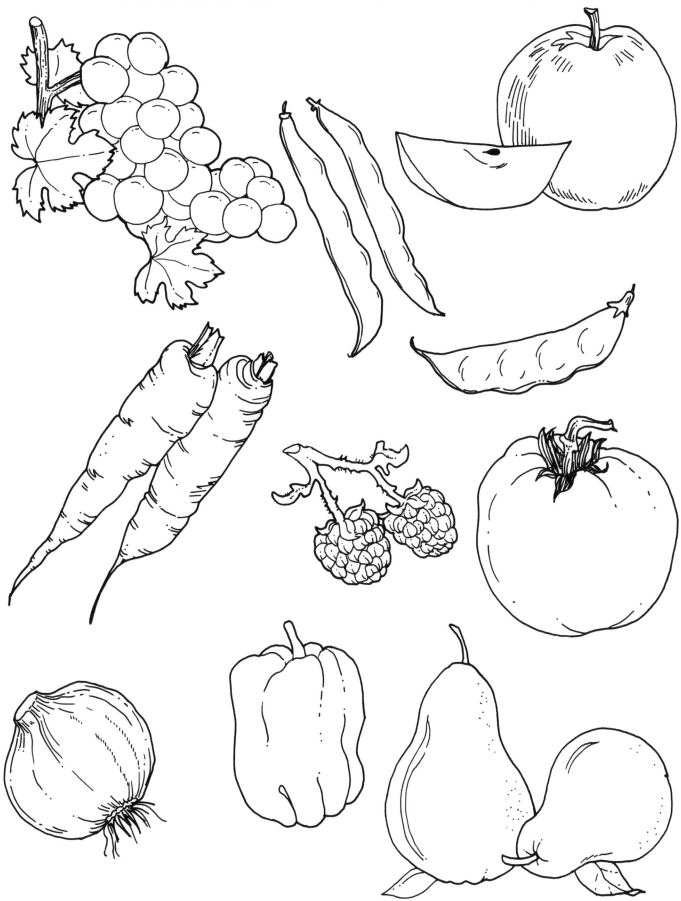

FINE FEATHERED FRIENDS

AUTUMN HARVEST

LEAVES

BUTTERNUT

DOGWOOD

OAK

COTTONWOOD

ELM

MAPLE

SEEDS

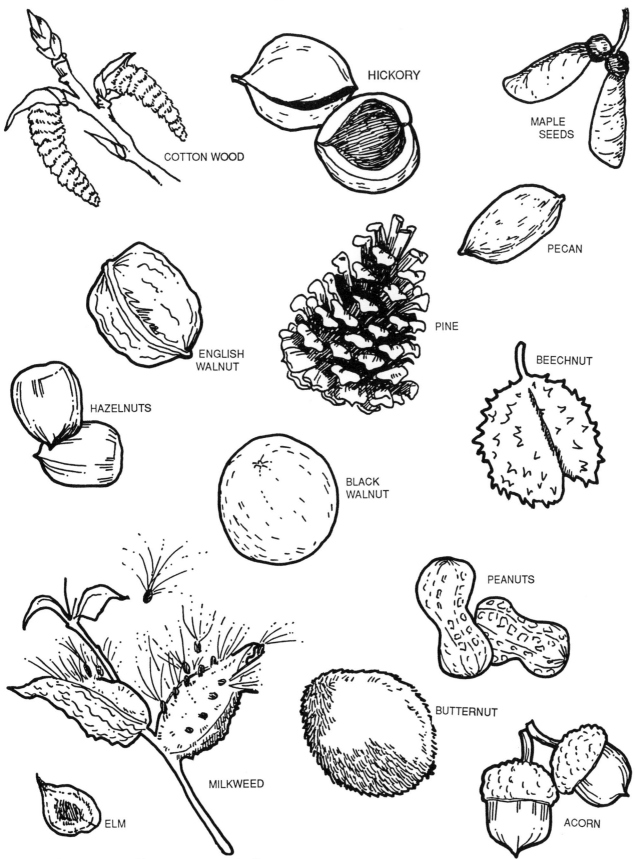

COTTON WOOD

HICKORY

MAPLE SEEDS

PECAN

ENGLISH WALNUT

PINE

BEECHNUT

HAZELNUTS

BLACK WALNUT

PEANUTS

BUTTERNUT

ELM

MILKWEED

ACORN

BUILDINGS

SCHOOL

PERSONALITY ANIMALS

DIZZY DINOSAURS

NOTES

THINGS TO DO

1. _____
2. _____
3. _____
4. _____
5. _____
6. _____
7. _____
8. _____
9. _____
10. _____
11. _____
12. _____
13. _____
14. _____
15. _____
16. _____
17. _____
18. _____
19. _____
20. _____
21. _____
22. _____
23. _____
24. _____
25. _____

A SPECIAL NOTE

Just Wanted You To Knooow...

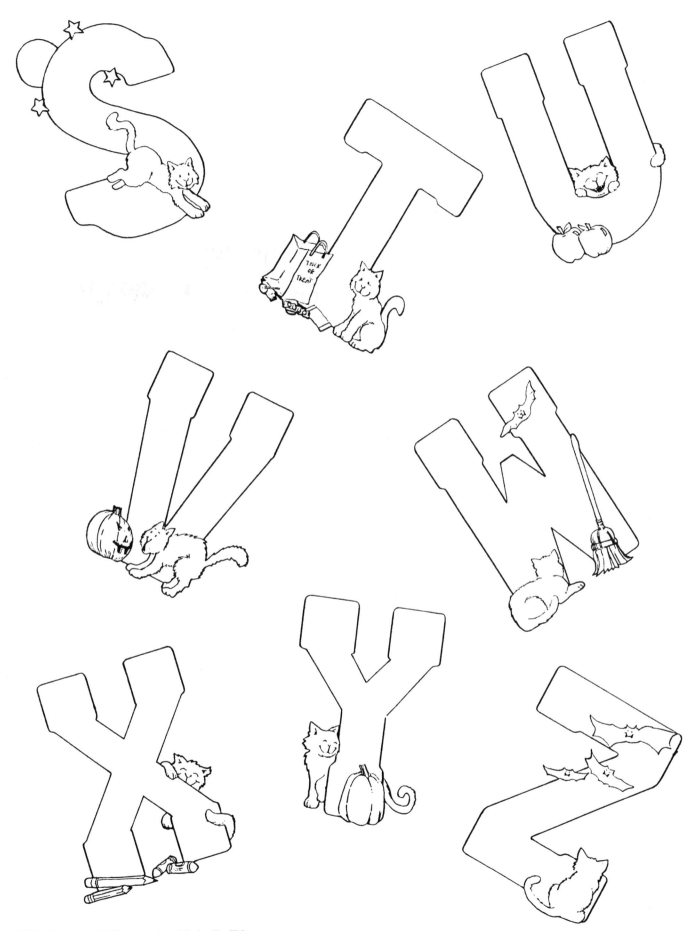